Jessie Norton

Heart's Ease and Other Verses

Jessie Norton

Heart's Ease and Other Verses

ISBN/EAN: 9783744665766

Printed in Europe, USA, Canada, Australia, Japan

Cover: Foto ©Thomas Meinert / pixelio.de

More available books at **www.hansebooks.com**

HEART'S EASE AND OTHER VERSES BY JESSIE NORTON

CLEVELAND: The Burrows Brothers Company, PUBLISHERS, MDCCC XCVIII

DEDICATION

This little book, O mother mine,
    I dedicate to thee,
For all the love and tender care,
    Thou hast bestowed on me.

CONTENTS

HEART'S EASE

When you've done the best you can, dear,
    And things go very wrong,
Don't pucker up your forehead,
    But sing a little song.
For maybe there's another
    Who's feeling just as sad,
And your little burst of music
    Might make him bright and glad.

Have you ever seen the pansies,
    Nod their heads low in the rain?
You think, when looking at them,
    They are very full of pain.
But these downcast little blossoms,
    With a more transparent hue,
Will lift their heads in beauty
    When the frowning skies are blue.

So oft our Heavenly Father
    Sends a little bit of woe,
To draw us nearer to Him,
    To make us pure, you know;
But He's such a tender Father,
    And He loves both me and you.
So He'll surely send His sunshine
    When the frowning skies are blue.

MY LITTLE GIRL

Of course the little girl was just as much of mine as
   hers,

But somehow, when our wedded life got full of
   pricks and burrs,

I told her that she'd better take the little one and go

And stay a spell at Newton creek, along with Uncle
   Jo,

While I'd go off to some far land and there I'd work
   and live

Until I'd quite made up my mind, which one was to
   forgive.

I tell you pride's an awful thing when it gets in the
   heart,

I guess it was a thousand times, I thought I'd rise
   and start

And go right after her and that little maid of mine.

I never heard a word from them, she never wrote a
   line,

Then I had a spell of sickness and counted through
   my tears,

And found I hadn't seen them both for more than
   fifteen years.

Oh, my pretty laughing darling, she must be tall
and fair!

How I'd rig her out in ribbons and feathers rich and
rare,

I could almost feel my fingers upon her soft white
brow,

That little sunny head of hers would touch my
shoulder now,

Yet the strangest thing, in all my dreams, she was a
little child,

With the yellow curls of babyhood and big eyes
round and mild.

As soon as I was better, I started on my way

And reached the town at noon-time, one hot and
dusty day,

And near by, in the church-yard, I stopped to rest
and wait,

There was a little baby's grave close to the mold'ring
gate;

I pushed aside a straggling vine, kind o' curious, no
more,

Great God, my little girl lay there, dead thirteen
years before.

MEMORIES

Just a little woman,
  Musing all alone —
Yet within the faded eyes
  A dim, sweet twilight shone.

Through the garret windows
  Streamed the sun's broad gold,
Lighting up the spinnet,
  Quaintly carved, of ancient mold.

Sitting there in silence,
  Her fingers on the keys,
Saw she wondrous visions
  Of gardens and green trees.

Heard she dreamy music
  Of songs, that he had sung,
Lingering near the spinnet,
  He, who had "died young."

Would he ever know her,
  Feeble, old, and gray?
His glad boyish beauty
  Had only seen life's day.

Ah, in God's own morning
　　She should be all fair —
Star eyes that ne'er would weary,
　　Soft bloom and golden hair.

Trembling, why she knew not,
　　With fingers ill at ease,
She struck the chords, then smiling,
　　Stooped and kissed the yellow keys.

AN OLD TIME SONG

A little old time song —
  Sung on a summer's day,
By children, whose wet feet
  Danced in the ocean's spray.
"Oh, little drops of dew,
  Oh, tiny grains of sand,
How small you are, but then
  You make the pleasant land."

The children played the while
  I measured in my soul
The little deeds of love,
  Yet what a mighty whole.
If every man would give
  Unto his neighbor's own,
A part of that true love
  He bears himself, alone.

Then through the realms of earth
  What songs of living peace,
For Christ, as King, would reign,
  The woes of all men cease —
Ah, tiny grains of sand,
  Do fill a shining space,
But little deeds of love,
  Lead to the Father's face.

IN THE AFTERWHILE

His little face was like a sun
  That shone into this soul of mine,
His baby laugh a thrilling run
  Of sweetest music, half divine.
E'en yet I see him standing near,
  I gaze into his steadfast eyes,
Which look, with vision bright and clear,
  On fairer things in Paradise.

Yet naught can part that boy from me,
  And when the years have run apace
I too, shall cross death's restless sea
  And look upon that little face.
And when I walk the hills of gold
  Which his white feet have ever trod,
My heart's full joy cannot be told,
  To know that he has lived with God.

THE YELLOW-HEADED BABY

When the yellow-headed baby came to Perkinses to
stay,

The children stuck their noses up and said they
wouldn't play.

They'd never waste vacation time attending likes of
him

From the very early morning until the stars were
dim.

They wondered what he came for, he wasn't wanted
there,

Nine of them a'ready and they hadn't room to spare.

He never owned a 'broidered slip or dainty ruffled
cap;

Was never crooned or cuddled down save in his
mother's lap.

A helpless, weakly little thing, who knew no love
but hers,

His life, a stony roadway, all bordered round with
burrs,

Until one sunny morning they found to their surprise

A boy a-toddling on his feet, with laughter in his
eyes.

Last week I saw the doctor's gig a-stopping at the
gate.

They'd evidently changed their minds, the boy was
now to wait,

And not go journeying off from them unto the hills
of God.

His tiny feet must walk the path his little brothers
trod.

And I heard the children crying, with a tear in every
eye —

"Oh, we're 'fraid our darling, darling little baby's
going to die."

This morning he was better, I met his father, Jim,

A big and burly carpenter, I saw his eyes were dim,

And his lips were all a-quivering as if with unknown
fears,

But oh, his eyes were shining and a-smiling through
his tears —

"I'm so glad, I cannot help it, for I heard the doctor
say,

That little yellow-headed chap of ours was going to
stay."

NOT AFRAID

My little maid
Was so afraid
Of shadows in the nursery room,
I used to feel
Her small arms steal
About me in the twilight gloom.

It fretted me
That she should see
The darker by-ways of this life;
Its bitter tears,
Its doubts and fears,
And agony and hopeless strife.

But pearly gates,
Where Gabriel waits,
Were opened for my darling sweet.
Yet heavenly bloom
Leads through the gloom
And who should guide her little feet?

When, lo, the child
Looked up and smiled,
She must have seen the angels nigh.
My little maid
Was not afraid —
Hush! do no cry.

MIRABEL'S GARDEN

"Mirabel, out in the garden,
   Down by the wicket gate,
What are you planting, my darling,
   In rows so cunning and straight?
Some little nut brown seedlings,
   Dropped into earth's dark gloom
To blossom in wonderful beauty,
   Long ere the summer's bloom."

Dear, little, wistful gardener —
   She lifted her face to mine,
And, lo, in the child eyes shining,
   Was the light of a love divine.
And, yet, as I bended o'er her,
   The strangest garden was seen,
For planted so deep and true and strong
   Were the tips of an evergreen.

Then, with her small face flushing,
   She answered me, grave and still,
"I am planting some baby Christmas trees
   For the children over the hill.
The poor little ragged children,
   Who never, never have known
What it was to dance round a Christmas tree
   All of their very own."

I snatched the child to my bosom
  And clasped her close to my breast.
My poor, little, dusty gardener,
  Who had done her very best!
And then with the tenderest caution
  I whispered what she didn't know;
That her Christmas trees for the children
  Would be scattered before the snow.

So oft on our weary journeyings
  Over this life of ours,
We scatter the seeds of a lavish love
  And never see the flowers.
Sometimes our brightest ambition
  Dwindles a candle spark,
And the deeds that we deem the truest
  Are hidden away in the dark.

And yet in His pitying mercy,
  God remembers we are but dust;
And though our mistakes be so many,
  Yet in Him if we put our trust,
Surely He'll guide and protect us
  Over life's turbulent seas;
And clasp us at last, as I did the child
  Who planted her Christmas trees.

AS HE SAW HER

His dear dead wife lay sleeping
  Beyond his loving call.
The gracious Lord had taken
  His dearest and his all.
For what were lands and children's
  Children, without her,
Who, through the wilderness of life
  Had strewn him balm and myrrh.

They saw him clasp within his own
  Her soft and withered hand,
And gaze at her half smiling —
  And they could not understand,
Unless he saw her waiting
  At the gates of Paradise,
White winged, in robes celestial,
  With holy radiant eyes.
Nay, nay, he saw no angel vision
  With starry crown,
But just a tender, girlish face
  With clinging locks of brown.

THE LITTLE SCHOOLMARM

I've done discussing schoolmarms, their punishments,
  and such,
And all their ways and doings don't fret me very
  much,
For I'd a true experience a year or two ago;
I learned a few things, gentlemen, that I was glad
  to know.

Our little lad came home from school, his eyes all
  wet with tears;
It took us half the noon-time to quiet down his fears.
He said that she had whipped him, that she was
  cross and old —
She never did a single thing but sit and fuss and
  scold.

The little one was innocent — I started for the school
To tell her who and what I was and lay her down a
  rule,
The afternoon was very hot, my temper hotter still,
And it had reached a boiling point when I had
  climbed the hill.

I had my speech all ready; I started for the door.
I guess she saw me coming, for she was there before,
And met me all a-smiling, with a welcome in her eyes.
I was the one to tremble, I found to my surprise.

The light was on her forehead, the light was on her
hair,
The light was all around her, like a glory everywhere.
Her eyes were like blue meadow flowers, we loved
when we were small,
Her gown, the self-same color, and she wasn't very
tall.

I couldn't say a single word, my throat was parched
and dry.
I nodded her, "Good afternoon," and slowly passed
her by,
"Come in and rest;" the sweetest voice that I had
ever heard.
The mingling of a baby's laugh and the singing of a
bird.

That night, 'twixt eight and nine o'clock, I let the
shingle fall,
And since that time we've never had a single fuss at
all.
So when you speak of schoolmarms as being cross
and bold,
She rises up before me, all shining blue and gold.

"*MUTATIO*"

Thus she came from heaven: Fair and sweet,
With tiny dimpled hands and rosebud feet.
A little maid with ever quest'ning eyes,
Of how or why she came from Paradise.
An earth-born child, yet portioned as to seem
An angel's second self or flitting dream.

Thus she entered heaven: Shy but wise,
With sweet snow face and gentle star-lit eyes,
Yet left behind a misty picture — rare,
With holy smiles and shining, shimmering hair —
All wrapped, yet seen, within a whirring cloud,
The living angel of our hearts' cold shroud.

AS A CHILD

A band of little scholars —
   Book and slate —
Each tiny hand must wield them
   Soon or late.
Yet what sweet knowledge
   Baby lips do bring,
Of flowers and great white stars,
   Of birds that sing.

A band of little scholars —
   With shut eyes,
Dreaming of wondrous things
   Beneath the skies.
Or looking unto worlds
   Not seen — afar —
Where God's white throne and countless
   Angels are.

A band of little scholars —
   Each will lose
That stern sweet purity;
   Yet one may choose
The narrow way — if be
   Through tempests wild,
And enter Heaven's gate —
   A little child.

COMFORT

I know that the sun is shining,
  That the fields are a-bloom with flowers,
Each swinging a dewy chalice
  Heavy with soft, warm showers.
I know that the robins are singing
  Their happiest lullabies,
But my heart is torn with the music —
  My nestling is in the skies.

Not with her coral and silver bells
  Doth my own little daughter stand,
She beareth a tall, white lily,
  Clasped in her tiny hand.
Not with her wee face dimpled,
  Tenderly raised to mine,
She gazeth with shy, new gladness
  Into the eyes divine.

All through the blush of the summer
  I guided her small white feet;
Now she hath heavenly teachers,
  And heavenly duties sweet.
Safe, safe 'neath their tender guidance,
  Away from earth's frost and shine,—
Thou wearest the crown of thine angelhood,
  Oh, dear little daughter mine!

CHRISTINA

How very, very sweet she is,
  How kind and true of manner,—
With gentleness, her only sword,
  And love, her golden banner.
We press her fingers and we feel
  New life — a charm is o'er us.
We gaze into her large clear eyes,
  And lo — the Light before us.

She hath a kindly love and care
  For all her neighbor creatures,
It brightens and makes glorified
  Her fair and girlish features.
We, wondering, do ask ourselves,
  "Of whence this power to win her?"
One answers, and we understand,
  "It is the Christ within her."

THE SMILING LITTLE FACES

I've been a long time traveling, I've crossed the
  ocean wide,
And gazed on many a curious thing upon the other
  side.
I've climbed the tower of Pisa and seen cathedrals
  old,
With their wondrous painted pictures and their cups
  of beaten gold.
But I'm weary, weary, longing for my mountains,
  grand and tall —
For the smiling little faces hanging on my parlor
  wall.

Strangers thought I was a bachelor, for I had no
  wife along,
And the women folks they smiled at me, of course,
  it wasn't wrong;
But somehow I couldn't tell them that where moun-
  tain roses blow
The one whom I had loved so well was lying cold
  and low,
With the little ones around her, just within her
  gentle call —
Oh, their bonny, bonny faces smiling on my parlor
  wall.

There was Bennie, little Bennie, with his dancing
eyes of brown,
Folks said he was the merriest chap they'd ever seen
in town;
And precious little Jackie, why he couldn't hardly
walk,
But he made such funny faces, said such pretty baby
talk;
And Cynthia, my Cynthia, she was growing fair and
tall,
And her sunny face still smiles at me down from the
parlor wall.

'Tis true 'tis God's own blessing in this world of woe
and sin,
When the clouds are hanging lowest, a little light's
let in.
I heard my neighbor's eldest boy, born 'long with
little Ben,
Declare himself in bitterness the wretchedest of men.
And Deacon Whipple's daughter, who used to play
with mine,
Has seen the saddest sorrows, does naught but fret
and pine.
So, I thank the gracious Father when the twilight
shadows fall
That they're safe, and I've their faces always smiling on the wall.

IN MEMORIAM

N. N. T.   (May, 1884.)

She slowly climbed the Ladder of Life,
  The misty, quiv'ring Ladder —
She entered upon its worldly strife,
  Just as the angels bade her.

She placed her foot on the first gold round,
  She followed sixteen after.
They've laid her low, in the damp cold ground,
  We miss her blithesome laughter.

Her gentle soul has wandered away,
  Far from the realms of sorrow,
It has reached the gates of lasting Day —
  The wonderful To-morrow.

HIS HAPPY FANTASY

"Haven't you seen a little lass
Trudging along through the prairie grass,
Say, boys, haven't you seen her pass
   Into the mining town?
I sent for her yesterday morn, you know,
I wanted to see her before I go;
She's my little queen, no scepter to show
   But the fluffiest curls for a crown.

"A kind little queen with a tender smile,
She loved me well all that terrible while
I was so wicked. She ran a mile
   For a kiss when I came away.
I have missed her so, I have missed her so.
'Tis almost a year — ten years? Ah, no!
My head is weak, it isn't that though,
   A year perhaps and — a day."

The old man sank with his failing eyes
Fixed as in hope on the sunset skies,
As if from their glory she'd surely rise
   And greet him with soft eyes mild.
He saw not the gleam of the heavenly gate,
Nor the countless angels that there await.
He only wondered why she was late,
   His beautiful, fair dream-child.

God's messenger stayed his sword of might,
In pity he folded his wings of white;
For, lo, at the first of the morning light
  The hut door was opened wide.
Ah, he had forgotten the years between;
No little round-faced maid was seen,
But a golden-haired girl of seventeen
  Crept to her father's side.

THE LITTLE GHOST

[C.M.B.C. (1830)]

A volume of yellow pages
    Writ in letters dim and fine,
Penned by the girlish fingers
    Of a dear little grandmother mine.
And oft in the shadowy twilight,
    As I sit with the book on my knee,
The fair little ghost of the writer
    Hastens to visit me.

Clad in a bygone fashion,
    Bright in ethereal bloom,
She comes with her star eyes shining,
    Into the darkening room,
And stands but a moment, expectant
    Of some chamber, I do not see,
And then with a soft little wistful sigh
    Drops by the book on my knee.

White are the shadowy fingers
    Tracing the letters dim,
Sweet is the voice of the little ghost
    Like the cadence of a hymn;
And I, who am only a stranger,
    Bend over the girlish head.
(I saw it again in my agony,
    Silent and gray and dead.)

Caroline, little ghost Caroline,
 Look into my face and see —
Not in a single feature
 Do I resemble thee.
Ah, but thy soft cheeks dimple,
 Thine eyes grow merry and glad,
Have I the face and the yellow hair
 Like his, thine own lover lad?

Brown are the eyes uplifted,
 Tender and true and sweet,
And I seem but an elder sister
 To this little ghost at my feet.
One, who never can know me,
 One, whom I never can know,
And she vanishes into the shadows
 When the first stars begin to glow.

Grandmother, dwelling in glory,
 When I have crossed death's sea,
Come not as this fair little phantom,
 Who cannot remember me.
But clad in a newer beauty
 And wrapped in a love divine,
Give me the welcome of heaven,
 Oh, blest little grandmother mine!

THE CANDLE LIGHT

You call him a drunken villain?
  Well, he isn't much to see.
A poor old man in his tattered clothes
  And as wretched as he can be.
Ah, why do I stand here pleading,
  I, who am spruce and tall?
I've known him, you see, for a long, long while,
  He's my father, that is all.

No, you wouldn't have owned him;
  I thought I wouldn't myself.
But somehow my brain ran rummaging round
  Over my memory's shelf.
And there was a thing that happened
  When I was a little lad,
(There wasn't a person in all the world
  Dearer to me than Dad).

A little sick boy and I lay one night,
  Alone in my trundle-bed.
And after a while Dad came over
  And stood at the cradle head,
And held a candle down in my face,
  And sobbed out wistfully,
"Oh, Dannie, my own little darlin' boy,
  Are you goin' away from me?"

All day, those words of my father
  Have pierced me through and through,
Till I had to come down to this wretched place
  And see what I could do;
For I know that the angels were watching,
  And God, too, saw the sight,
Of a little sick boy and his Daddy dear
  A-holding the candle light.

ANGELS OF GOD

'Tis said God's angels take no note of time,
The passing years glide by like some sweet chime.
They wait and sing before the shining One,
Yet tremble not; Earth's yesterdays are gone.

How strange it seems! We, too, weak as we are,
Shall wait and sing, each one like some white star,
In heavenly radiance, at the golden throne,
If we be the sweet Christ's and His alone.

DAY-DAWN

Oh Marguerite, wee Marguerite,
  She crept within the chancel old
And heard the anthem, soothing sweet,
  Of God's blest promise manifold.

"Ye weary pilgrim, do not weep,
  He will not, will not say thee nay,
The Lord his own dear child shall keep —
  'Tis darkest just before the day."

*   *   *   *

Ah, very dark for Marguerite,
  A starless sky; the snow-flakes fell
In glistening sandals for her feet,
  And clothed her white as asphodel.

Yet, through that waning wintry night,
  Her only coverlet the snow,
She had such wondrous visions bright,
  Of things unheard, unseen below.

The perfumed buds of lasting springs;
  Small cherub faces, coy and sweet,
The rush of many angels' wings —
  The day had dawned for Marguerite.

HIS LITTLE COMFORTER

He had left a darkened people
    And had reached his native land,
With a tired head, bowed and silvered,
    With an aged, trembling hand;
All the churches rang his praises,
    Yet he answered not a word,
They had given him the glory
    Which belonged unto his Lord.

And his heart was filled with trouble,
    And his old eyes dim with tears.
Had they all misunderstood him
    Through those long and weary years?
When up spoke a little maiden
    With a quaint and gracious air,
And he seemed to catch a glimmer
    Of God's sunshine in her hair.

"When I think of all those spirits
    That, through Christ, thou hast set **free**,
White-winged sentinels that ever
    Ope the pearly gates for thee;
How they'll shout their hallelujahs
    Mid the golden trumpet's din —
I should like to be in Heaven
    When God bids thee enter in!"

ACROSTIC

TO NELLIE.

Easter's holy joys be thine —
Azure skies and God's sunshine
Steal upon thee — bright and still,
Touching thy dear heart, until
Every sense of inward care
Rolls itself away in prayer.

THE SLEEPING BEAUTY

The charm was laid — that day
A little child, whose way
Led to a scepter's sway,
    Was doomed to sleep.
Not for eternity —
A hundred years should fly
In whose strong arms she'd lie
    In slumber deep.

Some day a prince would roam,
Far from his kingly home,
And hasten nigh and come
    To rescue her.
One kiss upon her brow —
But lo; the time is now,
The breezes come and go
    Like perfumed myrrh.

The master in his chair,
The page with flowing hair,
The holy monk at prayer,
    Close fast their eyes;
In turret chamber high,
That doth but touch the sky,
Without a smile or sigh,
    The princess lies.

The maid before the glass,
The rosy dairy lass,
The shades that come and pass,
   Stop short each task.
The horses in the stall,
The portraits on the wall,
The parrots in the hall,
   In sunshine bask.

About the oaken floor,
Around the castle door,
Where midnight tempests roar,
   An ivy grows.
On hidden treasure fair,
On jewels, soft and rare,
On powdered, gem-strewn hair,
   The gray dust shows.

One day a prince full young,
From tow'ring hedge-row sprung,
The startled echoes rung
   In hollow tone.
One step upon the stair,
One kiss on forehead fair,
And waking life is there,
   Not slumb'ring stone.

FOR LITTLE SCHOLARS

COUSIN ANN ELIZA'S SCHOOL

I get so very, very tired —
  We dare not turn our heads around,
We have to sit so still and straight
  And never make the leastest sound.
So often, though I know it's wrong,
  When Miss Bedell explains a rule,
I think of Uncle David's farm
  And Cousin Ann Eliza's school.

She opens all the windows wide,
  So we can hear the robins sing;
We swing our feet and clap our hands,
  She doesn't mind our whispering;
And when our heads get very tired,
  We bow them down to rest, you know,
She never cares but only smiles —
  She loves her little scholars so.

And just as soon as school is out,
  (We never have to stay for her)
We rush to get the ginger cake
  That Aunt Maria likes to stir.
Then on the door-step we sit down
  And laugh and sing and shout and play,
I am so happy all the time,
  I never wish for Saturday.

My mother heard me telling once
  About this jolly little school,
She opened wide her eyes and said,
  "I'm 'fraid Ann doesn't teach by rule."
I never said a single word,
  Yet all the happy summer long,
We never spell a reader through,
  Or learn the first verse of a song.

A KIND LITTLE SOUL

The little birds do sing within the garden all the day,
I hear them sweetly chirping when I am at my play;
But I never, never think of hurting them, you know,
Because they are God's creatures and I'm sure he
loves them so.

There is a small gray kitten in the yard, just back
of us,
And when she sees me coming she makes the greatest
fuss
To hide behind the cellar steps and jump and frighten
me;
I think that little kitten 'bout as cunning as can be.

And yesterday, by our front gate, was Tommy
Tucker's dog,
Pretending that he was asleep and lying like a log;
But when he heard me coming he pricked his ears
up so,
Because I always pat his head and stroke his face,
you know.

When I am tall like father and wear a high black hat,
I know I'll never change my mind about a dog or cat,
Or any other creature in earth or sea or sky,
They'll never need to fear a thing when I am pass-
ing by.

SPRING SONG

Hark the robins sweetly sing —
List and hear the bluebells ring —
Little Mayflowers, swinging low
Your pale faces to and fro,
Whispering softly, "Come and see,
We the children's friends will be,
Close beside the sheltering grass,
Stoop and pluck us as you pass.

"White and cold, the falling snow,
Loud, the rough north winds did blow,
But beneath our blanket white,
Slept we through the wintry night,
Till we heard the robins sing,
Whispered we 'It is the Spring,'
And we oped our sleepy eyes
For the children's glad surprise."

UNAPPRECIATED

I stood "one hundred" on my slate —
　　That was the best in all our row.
But I'm a little orphan girl,
　　There's only grandmamma to know;
And she is very old and blind,
　　And doesn't seem to understand.
So I just kiss her wrinkled cheek
　　And try to smooth her poor thin hand.

When Dottie Kirby is the best,
　　Her papa takes her on his knee,
And slips a penny in her hand,
　　Then kisses her right merrily.
And little Johnnie's mother makes
　　A ginger cookie man for him.
I know she does, for once I had
　　A bite from off his broad hat's brim.

So, often, when I feel so sad,
　　I go to where my papa lies.
My mamma, too, is sleeping there.
　　And then I look into the skies
And wonder if the angels see;
　　Or if they ever think to say,
"That little daughter whom you left,
　　Has done her very best to-day."

"THREE"

Such a funny little fellow
With a funny little face!
And he wore a checkered collar
All embroidered 'round with lace.

He was chirp as any cricket,
And the first at bat and ball,
But when it came to lessons —
Well, he wasn't there at all.

So one pleasant day, the teacher
Told the children they should spell,
Wrote "to" upon the blackboard,
"To," they answered right and well.

"Now I'll add another 'o,' dears;
"What's the word?   Why, don't you see?"
And this funny little fellow,
With a chuckle, answered, "Three!"

HYMN FOR CLOSE OF SCHOOL

What have the children been doing to-day?
Tell me, O little folks, what do you say?
We minded our teacher, and sat up quite straight,
And always were busy with pencils and slate,
Read pretty lessons and sang a nice tune;
Now at the end of this bright afternoon
We'll bow down our heads, and then softly we'll say,
"We thank Thee, dear Lord, for this beautiful day."

THE LEAF BUD

Oh, queer little nut-brown cradle,
  Swinging on yonder tree.
'They have told me the strangest secret,
  A most wonderful mystery!
I thought that the dull, bare branches
  Tossing against the sky
Were dead, but I know they will blossom
  Into beauty, by and by.

Oh, dear little nut-brown cradle,
  You treasure a tiny leaf,
Only your nursling's babyhood
  Is very, very brief.
But out of the blasts of winter,
  The icy sleet and the cold,
Safe, safe 'neath the soft brown coverlet,
  The dear, little leaf you hold.

Till kissed by the warm spring sunshine
  And rocked by the breezes sweet.
Lo, the little brown cradle is wafted
  Down to my very feet.
But where is the tender nursling?
  In garments of living green,
Held close, so close, to the old tree's breast
  The fair little leaf is seen.

FINGER EXERCISE

Ten little birds in the summer sky,
What are you doing up so high?
Ten little birds came down to see
What in the world the matter could be.
Ten little birds flew up again,
Swallow and sparrow, robin and wren.
But as I watched them they soared away,
And left me alone that summer day.

Ten little fingers, high in the air,
Listen, you'll hear them snapping up there.
Ten little fingers, quiet and small,
Hearken, you cannot hear them at all.
One little body, standing so straight,
One little heart, made to love, not to hate.
One little daughter, or one little son —
Be seated, dear children, our frolic is done.

OUT OF THE WINDOW

[*Exercise Song*]

Out of the window, over the way,
Saw I a cobbler, mending to-day;
Thump went the hammer on Sallie's shoe,
"Humph," said the cobbler, "I guess you will do."

Out of the window, over the way,
Saw I a tailor, sewing to-day.
How did he do it? Why to and fro
Ran his great needle through the cloth, — so.

Out of the window, over the way,
Saw I the children in school, to-day.
What were they doing? Why, don't you know?
Writing straight letters on pages of snow.

Out of the window, over the way,
Soon will be closing the gates of the day;
Then will the children, in robes of white,
Sleepily murmur, "Good night, all, good night."

ACROSTIC

["*Columbus*"]

[*Exercise for eight children bearing letters composing acrostic*]

C's for Columbus, so gallant and bold,
O's for the Ocean, that tumbled and rolled,
L's for the Light, dimly seen on the shore,
U's the Unkindness, which Columbus bore,
M's for his Memory, beaming and bright,
B's for the Birth of a new world of light —
U's for our Union, oh, long may it stand,
S for the Shores of our dear native land.

All

Now, children, look quickly and tell if you can
What is the name of this wonderful man.

GAME TO TEACH FIVE

One little cat in the corner,
  Washing her furry face.
One little cat comes to catch her;
  Two little cats run a race.

Two little cats in the corner,
  Each with her own plump mouse.
One comes in from the door-yard;
  Three little cats in the house.

Three little cats on the doorstep,
  Warming themselves in the sun.
One comes up from the cellar;
  Four little cats,— such fun!

Four little cats by the window,
  Watching the twilight's ray.
One jumps out of the basket;
  Five little cats end the day.

THE NAUGHTY KITTY

Little stranger, have you pity
For a naughty little kitty,
Who would not mind his dear mamma at all?
But he was so very pretty,
Such a roly poly kitty —
When he slept he looked just like a soft gray ball.

But he wouldn't mind his mother,
And he taught his little brother
How to tease and scratch the other, don't you see?
Now the other was a sister,
When he scratched her, a great blister
Came upon her paw, a cruel thing, ah me!

So his mother wouldn't hold him,
And she put him in the cold, dim
Cellar, in the corner, every day,
Till the naughty little kitty,
Oh the pity, oh the pity,
Crept beneath the cellar door and ran away.

'Round and 'round the great, great city,
Ran the frightened little kitty,
Till again he reached his own beloved door.
Then with sighing and with sobbing,
And with little heart a-throbbing,
He vowed he'd mind his mother evermore.

CHRISTMAS RHYME

The beauties of the Christmas tree
  Are known both far and wide,
    Its candles bright,
    Its balls of light,
  And many things beside.

I see a dolly swinging there,
  In robe of azure blue,
    A painted sled,
    A top of red —
  I'm sure these are for you.

I asked Santa the other day,
  If he would bring to me —
    A parasol
    For my best doll,
  And china for my tea.

And Bennie wants a worsted dog,
  But it must bark and run;
    I could have named,
    (But was ashamed)
  A thousand things and one.

The beauties of the Christmas tree
Are known both far and wide,
Its candles bright,
Its balls of light,
And many things beside.

THE BABY'S VISIT

Once there was a baby,
 So I've heard it told,
Eyes of deepest azure,
 Hair of ruddy gold;
And she paid a visit
 To a little school,
Where the gentle teacher
 Taught the Mystic Rule.

Everything seemed wondrous
 To the baby's eyes;
Everything the children did
 Filled her with surprise.
"Write, my little scholars,
 Patiently and slow,
You shall name the prettiest slates,
 When we marching go."

Ah, life's veriest sunshine
 Filled each little face,
And the pointed pencils
 Moved with patient grace.
But the baby's letters
 Wouldn't stand up straight,
Oh, the crooked pot-hooks
 On her little slate.

This one named his sweetheart,
  This her little beau;
But the fair child visitor
  Had no one, you know.
So when she was questioned,
  Azure eyes a-shine.
Answered, "All are pitty,
  But the pittiest one is mine."

ACROSTIC

["*Christmas*"]

C is for Christmas, most holy and bright,
H for the Happiness, born of delight,
R for the Ringing of bells, sweet and clear,
I for the Interest God has in us here,
S for the Star, shining bright in the sky,
T for the Tidings, sent forth from on high,
M for the Morning, most glorious of all.
A for the Angels who sang at his call,
S for the Savior, asleep in the stall

EXERCISE SONG

Air: "*The Whistling Coon*"

Sing, sing, oh, what shall I sing?
My little kitty sang a pretty tune,
  She opened wide her jaws,
  And clapped her tiny paws,
She did so well I gave her a gold spoon.

Chorus:

  Left, right, rest together now,
    Raise your heels and clap your little hands;
  Turn, bow, all erect once more.
    Oh, how well each little scholar stands!

Sing, sing, oh, what shall I sing?
I heard a gentle tapping at the door;
  There stood a snowy pig,
  Who danced a funny jig,
From half past seven until nearly four.

                            Chorus.—

Sing, sing, oh, what shall I sing?
I know one of the dearest little schools,
  Where all the children work
  And never, never shirk,
And everybody minds the teacher's rules.

                            Chorus.—

THE LESSON OF THE ANTS

I didn't want to go to school,
I hated ev'ry single rule,
And so I took my picture book,
And went down by the meadow brook,
And sat myself beneath a tree,
And spread the book upon my knee.
But then I couldn't read, you know,
Because the sunbeams flickered so,
And casting my two eyes around,
I saw the ants upon the ground,
All making nests within the sand,
Oh, what a merry, busy band!
There wasn't one who stopped to play,
They worked and worked and worked away,
And this is what I heard them say,
"Fie, naughty child, to run away,
For Time is ever on the wing,
He doesn't wait for anything."

I was ashamed to think that I
Who knew much better, shouldn't try.
And so I shut my picture book
And left that lovely meadow brook,
With all its sunshine and its birds
And went to school to study words.

I learned my lessons o'er and o'er
Much better than I had before
Until the letters seemed to dance,
And then they looked like little ants,
And this is what I heard them say,
"O little scholar, work away,
For Time is ever on the wing,
He doesn't wait for anything."